QUAGGA

Aaron Carr

www.av2books.com

LET'S READ
AV²
BY WEIGL™
ADDED VALUE • AUDIO VISUAL

Go to **www.av2books.com**, and enter this book's unique code.

BOOK CODE

J557477

AV² by Weigl brings you media enhanced books that support active learning.

AV² provides enriched content that supplements and complements this book. Weigl's AV² books strive to create inspired learning and engage young minds in a total learning experience.

Your AV² Media Enhanced books come alive with...

Audio
Listen to sections of the book read aloud.

Video
Watch informative video clips.

Embedded Weblinks
Gain additional information for research.

Try This!
Complete activities and hands-on experiments.

Key Words
Study vocabulary, and complete a matching word activity.

Quizzes
Test your knowledge.

Slide Show
View images and captions, and prepare a presentation.

... and much, much more!

Published by AV² by Weigl
350 5th Avenue, 59th Floor
New York, NY 10118

Websites: www.av2books.com   www.weigl.com

Library of Congress Control Number: 2014958635
ISBN 978-1-4896-3082-7 (hardcover)
ISBN 978-1-4896-3083-4 (softcover)
ISBN 978-1-4896-3084-1 (single-user eBook)
ISBN 978-1-4896-3085-8 (multi-user eBook)

Printed in the United States of America in Brainerd, Minnesota
1 2 3 4 5 6 7 8 9 0 19 18 17 16 15

022015
WEP021315

Project Coordinator: Aaron Carr
Art Director: Terry Paulhus

All illustrations by Jon Hughes, pixel-shack.com. Photos: page 20–21, Alamy.

EXTINCT ANIMALS QUAGGA

In this book, you will learn

what its name means

what it looked like

where it lived

what it ate

and much more!

Meet the quagga.
Its name comes from
the sound it made.

4

Quaggas were the same size as the zebras of today.

They could weigh
up to 700 pounds.

Quaggas had stripes that only covered part of their bodies. Each quagga had a different pattern of stripes.

Quaggas were plant eaters.
They spent their days eating
in fields of long grass.

Quaggas could run quickly on their four long legs. They could run up to 35 miles an hour.

Quaggas lived in family groups called harems.

Harems sometimes joined to make large herds.

Quaggas lived
in southern Africa.

They mostly roamed across grasslands.

Quaggas died out more
than 100 years ago.

The last quagga
died in a zoo
in 1883.

19

Today, people can go to museums to learn more about the quagga.

QUAGGA FACTS

These pages provide detailed information that expands on the interesting facts found in the book. They are intended to be used by adults as a learning support to help young readers round out their knowledge of each amazing animal featured in the *Extinct Animals* series.

Pages 4–5

The name quagga comes from the sound the animal made. The quagga was once thought to be a distinct species, but scientists now classify it as a subspecies of the plains zebra. The word *quagga* most likely comes from an imitation of the braying sound the animal made. It is believed to have come from the language of the indigenous Khoikhoi people of southwestern Africa. There was only one subspecies of quagga, known as the true quagga. Its scientific name was *Equus quagga quagga*.

Pages 6–7

Quaggas were about the same size as modern-day zebras. The quagga stood about 4 feet (1.3 meters) tall at the withers. The withers is the highest point of a zebra's back. It weighed between about 500 and 700 pounds (226 and 317 kilograms). This is within the size range of the present-day plains zebra, which can be from 3.5 to 5 feet (1.1 to 1.5 m) tall and weigh 440 to 990 pounds (200 to 450 kg).

Pages 8–9

Quaggas looked different from modern-day zebras. The quagga only had stripes on its head and upper body. The head had the typical black and white stripes, but the rest of the body was a yellowish-brown color. Black stripes ran down the neck to the shoulders, and sometimes to part of the back. The legs were white, with no striping. Each quagga had a stripe pattern that was unique to that particular animal, similar to fingerprints in humans.

Pages 10–11

Quaggas were herbivores, or plant-eaters. Like modern-day zebras, quaggas were nomadic grazing animals. This means they moved from place to place in search of grass to graze. They sought fields of long grass for daytime feeding and retreated to areas of shorter grass at night. The short grass made it more difficult for predators to sneak up on them. In addition to grass, quaggas may have also eaten leaves and plant stems.

Pages 12–13

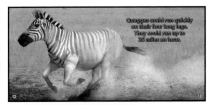

Quaggas could run up to 35 miles (56 kilometers) per hour. Similar to other kinds of plains zebras, the quagga had adapted to outrun its predators. Predators included various African big cats, such as lions and leopards, as well as hyenas. If predators came too close to the quagga, it could defend itself by kicking with its long, powerful hind legs. Quaggas were always on the move. They covered as much as 10 miles (16 km) each day.

Pages 14–15

Quaggas lived in family groups called harems. A harem was usually made up of a single adult male, or stallion, and several adult females, or mares. Offspring, called foals, were also a part of the harem. The male was the primary leader and protector of the harem. A harem could have a home range as small as 11 square miles (30 square kilometers) or as large as 232 square miles (600 sq. km) for migratory harems.

Pages 16–17

Quaggas lived in southern Africa. They mostly lived in grassland and savanna habitats that ranged from temperate to dry. However, they sometimes roamed into wetter environments. The quagga was the southernmost dwelling of all plains zebras. They were found throughout the area of the modern-day country of South Africa. Their range extended south from the Orange River and Vaal River and west of the Drakensberg escarpment.

Pages 18–19

Quaggas died out more than 100 years ago. The last quagga died on August 12, 1883, at a zoo in Amsterdam, Netherlands. It was not known until years later that this had been the last quagga on Earth. The quagga was hunted to extinction in its natural habitat. Throughout the 1800s, South Africa was known around the world as a "hunter's paradise." This, combined with local farmers who considered the quagga a pest, led to the animal's extinction.

Pages 20–21

People can go to museums to learn more about the quagga. Each year, millions of people see quaggas displayed in museums around the world. These displays may be either complete or partial skeletons. Often, displays consist of life-sized recreations made using preserved skins. In the United States, the Peabody Museum of Natural History in New Haven, Connecticut, and the Academy of Natural Sciences in Philadelphia, Pennsylvania, each have quagga exhibits.

KEY WORDS

Research has shown that as much as 65 percent of all written material published in English is made up of 300 words. These 300 words cannot be taught using pictures or learned by sounding them out. They must be recognized by sight. This book contains 49 common sight words to help young readers improve their reading fluency and comprehension. This book also teaches young readers several important content words, such as proper nouns. These words are paired with pictures to aid in learning and improve understanding.

Page	Sight Words First Appearance	Page	Content Words First Appearance
4	comes, from, it, its, made, name, sound, the	4	quagga
6	as, of, same, were	6	size, zebras
7	could, they, to, up	7	pounds
8	a, different, each, had, only, part, that, their	8	bodies, pattern, stripes
10	days, in, long, plant	10	eaters, fields, grass
13	an, four, miles, on, run	13	hour, legs
14	family, groups, lived	14	harems
15	large, make, sometimes	15	herds
18	more, out, than, years	16	Africa
19	last	17	grasslands
20	about, can, go, learn, people	19	zoo
		20	museums